Are You Who You "Post" To Be? : Finding Your True Identity in God

Danita Ogandaga

www.danitaogandaga.com

Danita Ogandaga

Are You Who You "Post" To Be:

Finding Your True Identity In Christ

Published by: Danita Ogandaga

www.danitaogandaga.com

Please visit www.danitaogandaga.com for more information
on purchasing bulk copies and requests for book translation.

Unless otherwise indicated, "Scripture quotations taken
from the New American Standard Bible®, Copyright © 1960,
1962, 1963, 1968, 1971, 1972, 1973,
1975, 1977, 1995 by The Lockman Foundation
Used by permission." (www.Lockman.org)

retrieval system without the expressed written permission of the author, except for the inclusion of brief quotations in a review.

Disclaimer and/or Legal Notices

The information presented herein represents the views of the author as of the date of publication. Because of the rate with which conditions change, the author reserves the right to alter and update her opinions based on the new conditions.

Table of Contents

Forward

I'll always remember the first day that I met Danita. We were introduced at the fountain at our college, the University of North Carolina at Greensboro. It was a brief encounter and I really liked the way that she looked. She was very pure and beautiful and I could see the light in her eyes that translated fearlessness and much vision.

Are You Who You "Post" To Be?

She invited us that same night to come to her poetry readings on campus. When we got to the event, I was amazed by the passion and organization as well as the amounts of people whom she pulled from Raleigh, Durham, campus, as well as the community to attend this event. I was extremely impressed by that because I have been looking for a woman who already had her own influence. I knew where I was going in life and I did not need just a cute lady with no substance.

When you read this book, I do not want you to think that Danita wrote this book from a few Google searches, but this book represents a small portion of the amount of resources and experiences she has on identity and purpose. She has been on this journey of practicing and helping people discover their identity to launch their purpose for 19 years.

Yes, she has a degree, many of them; but this book is beyond having degrees. She is talking from her soul and her spirit first so the authenticity of her message will not let somebody in search of who they are be lost.

If you are looking for your true self and not who you are posting on social media. this book will guide you towards who you truly are at your core.

Darcy Ogandaga

Trillionaire Media Inc.

Danita's Husband and Boyfriend For Life

Thank You

Darcy Ogandaga- Thank you. You have never allowed me to stop fulfilling the purpose that God put on the inside of me and I thank you for that. Your love has ministered to me in the most challenging times. You are an excellent husband and father to our girls. We are simply blessed to have you.

Talmer-Marie and Boutou Sudie Ogandaga- My sweet babies, I love you so much. From the time that I felt you kicking in my womb, I knew that you were special gifts given to us by Jesus himself. I am so glad that I get to be your mom and guide you back into the love of Father God. I pray you take hold of the promise of knowing how special and thought of you are by God. He loves you so much.

Family and Friends That Are Family- I thank you for pouring into my when I need it most. Octavia Roberts, Nikkia Thiam, and Djakarta Solomon Lynch you know how you do!

GriefTalk Clients, Trillionaire Media, & Our Social Media Following- Thank you for supporting Darcy and I over the years and purchasing our products, sowing into our travels and engagements, and simply taking the time to equip yourselves with becoming knowledgeable about the purpose of social media. This work is a ministry that we take very seriously. We love you all.

Are You Who You "Post" To Be? : Finding Your True Identity in God

A Cracked Perspective

That moment you realize you've been sleeping and the alarm clock is still ringing. Suddenly, you wake up from your sleep and wipe your eyes as you ask yourself the question, " How did I get to this place in my life?"

Let me remind you of an important fact, unlike the person who's Facebook status you just checked that may be still wondering how they are going to keep up with the façade they are projecting on social media, the difference is, this, my dear, is your life, are you who you were supposed to be?

Challenging all that I believe and reaching a point that you know in your life despite all that you have been exposed to all of your life, sitting under from the pews of the church, and all that has been circulating in your mental filter from traditions, religion, and familiarity, you know that you have reached the point where something is prompting you and letting you know that something is off, something is not working. In all of your efforts to be normal, you must answer the call to abandon mediocre, flee freedom in finding your own path, clip the strings on having your way, and accept the fact that your bags are too heavy, your perspective is cracked, and you must accept the invitation to shift your mindset.

I sat down to write this book a year ago excited about the awesome opportunity Father God had given me to create a positive impact in the life of my brother and sister and then out of nowhere it felt as though I was hit by a freight train. When you make a decision to follow the path of God's plan for your life and abandon your hopes, dreams, desires, and wants, you must be prepared to know that God will take you where he needs you to go. There, it may not always feel good or be what you want to be exposed or exposed to, but the goodness in it all, is that you will step forth free and able to walk in your truth and in the freedom that God has as you being his child.

Shortly after receiving the topic for this book, my husband and I were blessed with the awesome news that on the same day of finding out my only sister, a three time breast cancer survivor, and her husband were pregnant, we were pregnant also. After waiting five years and wondering if it would ever happen, we were elated that our family would be welcoming a new life into our family.

Are You Who You "Post" To Be?

Beginning the process of getting our household, schedule, and life ready for a new one, we booked a photography session with one of Atlanta's top photographers, paid a retainer, and selected the venue. The morning of the photo shoot, the weather was beautiful, we were excited, and to move things forward, the photo shoot was beautiful. We had signs made that Baby Ogandaga was coming. The elation in our 5 year old daughter's eyes was priceless, after all, she was going to get her wish of having a life size human doll in the house to play with.

Weeks later, we had gotten the pictures back and the day before we were to release the pictures to our family and sharing with our business clients on our social media networks, we found ourselves in the hospital telling us the sac was emptying and the process of a miscarriage had begun. Refusing to have surgery on that morning, we went home and prayed believing that God would answer our request for saving our baby. Despite the prayers, we ended up back at the hospital that evening and I was being rolled into surgery to remove the residue of the baby that remained from the pregnancy.

We were so devastated, partly because several weeks before, my sister and her husband had also found out that they had lost their baby. No pictures would go out, no announcement would be shared, because miscarriages are not a recognized death by many, my husband and I retreated to our home for the healing to begin in the presence of close friends and family.

During the next week, taking time to heal and get before Father God, he let me know in a small voice, "You will not be any good to anyone if you do not lighten your load that you are carrying. Give the pain to me, I am able to support it. I can handle it all. Give it to me. I am your Father God and I love you so much." I felt myself get angry and lighter at the same time recognizing that this tragedy was clearly a theft, I ran to the word and decided to get filled with the promises of God.

I wanted to find a target that would tangibly pay for the theft that had been enforced upon me as well as my sister but getting upset at the doctors and medical field would not do. I turned to Father God and began to build my faith. Taking the stack of pictures from our photo shoot, well over $2,000 in price, and began cutting them up while crying. I was broken and I needed God to help mend me back together again.

Since I own GriefTalk and have a steady stream of clients, I received instructions to source my clients out while I healed from my own grief. In doing so, and surprisingly to me, I began to receive a stream of calls from people specifically needing assistance and healing work in the area of stillborn, miscarriages, and post-abortions. I cried out to the Father asking him why he would send people to me in my state of brokenness. He constantly told me that he was going to get the glory for everything that was happening in my life as well as theirs. It was at that moment that he took me to Isaiah 54:1 that said "Sing barren woman, you who have no children, sing."

For some time now within the grief work that I do, I involve narrative therapy which encourages my clients to write as a means of healing. Sharing that message, I too began to see the hand of God equip me with instruction for these women and men in the midst of their situation. Father God loving me so much like he did, also aided me and my family in our hurt and I began to see my perspective change. Why would the God I love so much cause me to undergo this great pain of losing a child? It was so difficult for me to grasp but I realized that in the midst of it all, he loved me still and wanted to know that he would ensure that I would recover all.

He instructed me one night to take the picture of my husband, Tally, and I sitting on a fountain holding a sign that our baby was coming June 2014. He told me to cut the date out and trust that he would restore me before the end of the year. Thinking the restoration would come in some other form other than the painful desire of getting pregnant again, I began to thank God for increase not once thinking that it would be a baby. See, I shut my mindset off to believe that although I wanted a baby and had received instructions telling me that he would recover all, I wanted to continue carrying the weight of myself that I could not produce another pregnancy but how many of you know God can!

Shortly after cutting the date out of the picture, I put it on my wall and began to look at it daily thanking God that he would restore what the enemy stole. Then the day came, when I was headed to pick my daughter up from school. I heard Father God say to me, "Do you believe that I can restore you?" I said, "God, I do believe, help me to know that you love me and even if you never give us a baby, it is not because you cannot." Well how many of you know that once you bear down in faith like that, Father God will meet you right where you are, even if you are in the pits of doubt and unbelief, he will help you. Three months later, while doing the keynote at a Women's Conference, we found out we were pregnant with our baby girl, Boutou-Sudie, meaning, "Child of Promise"!

Lessening the load is what this book is about. Learning that we have stuff and for many of us, that stuff needs to be sorted and a decision made whether to keep, donate, or trash what we have in our hands tangibly or within the depths of our mindset which frame the essence of who we are.

The Crisis

One question comes to mind that may take you on a journey over the next few hours, days, weeks, or however long it takes you to read this book. Every fiber of your being may go back to the days of Tonka, Spiderman, watching Fat Albert, or the Cosby Show and Ninja Turtles or Barbie, Wonderwoman, or that thing that you connected with when you were a child that made you feel invincible.

The Art of Remembering

Can you remember who you were before the world told you

who should be?

We have been given victory over every obstacle that

we face. Those things that we are going through right now

do have an expiration date and praise belongs to God. The

bible declares this over and over. There is nothing like

understanding what you are dealing with so you will know how to attack the issues that are attacking you. In this chapter we will talk about a few areas in our life that have caused great concern, delay, and pause in pursuing the goals that God has given us to do. As we read over each section, I want you to be mindful that from the very start, your goal is victory. Even though you may be in the thick of your mess, knee deep in the dramas of your past and present, you CAN overcome everything that you are faced with.

Selfie Generation

A selfie as defined by Merriam Webster is an image of oneself taken using a digital camera especially for posting on social networks. A global phenomenon, it was interesting during my research to find the history that connects the dots on this issue. There was a man, a young man named Narcissus, who was what one would called fine. Loved by all the nymphs in his circle, he is not quite sure why he is loved so much. Wanting to be alone, he retreats to the woods, thirsty, he approaches a body of water and leans over to drink it. Seeing the reflection of his face in the mirror, he falls madly in love with himself. The major obstacle that he encounters is that he is unable to tangibly possess the thing that he loves the most; his image.

As a result, in sorrow, he refrains from nurture, no sleeping, no eating, he dies. Some researchers point narcissism to the acquisition of being so busy with creating an image for yourself that you ultimately become emotionally empty. From Freud to other psychological bodies of work, even that of the American Psychiatric Association's *Diagnostic and Statistical Manual of Mental Disorders*, also referred to as the DSM-V, refer to the condition being associated with the idea of being grand in life: special person, special status, special privileges, special everything feeling little to no concern for others, both envying them as well as believing you are envied as well.

Tell me, how can anyone get anything done when you are constantly envying others through your own insecurity and not owning when you are envying them. Blah...Blah...Blah..... the synopsis of that is this: when it comes down to paper, therapists, the difference between them and social media is perception: judgment versus concern. The reality is, the generation of the selfie is one where many will look to others to find if they are tolerant when the real issue is that they are sick with themselves.

I am not saying that the rise of selfies have created an influx in the diagnosis of personality disorders, but what I am saying is that when you look at the image that is portrayed in the taking of a selfie, the perception is that this image is one that is frozen and unable to change or be altered and frankly, this is the unfortunate mindset that many are operating in today: they are uncertain that who they are desiring to become based on their experiences in life is enough to match or compare to the person that they once were or are tired of being. Asking, " Who Am I Now?" This question keeps them FROZEN in despair, because if you are so focused on coming out of who you were or are tired of being, how can you possibly began to put the pieces of thought together for who you are wanting to be now?

Despite what you may be thinking or what you may have read, I want you to sow Genesis 1:31 into your spirit because it is an expression for the way that Father God sees you. It says, " And God saw everything that he had made and said, Behold, it is very good." And God entered into his rest.

When we are constantly wondering and worrying who we are and what others think about us, we open the door to worry, fear, dread, doubt, insecurity, and all the cousins that follow in that family. You can't possibly sleep at night or be productive during the day when you ALWAYS feel as though there is something missing from your life. Not being able to put a finger on how you are feeling is one of the worst things that can further frustrate your journey because in all your knowing that something is wrong, you are unable to articulate what the WRONG is.

This uncertainty breeds broke relationship and uncertainty over who you are. Your relationships may suffer because a part of you is willing to uphold the selfie in the picture and what that has come to mean for you, your family, your friends, your peers, your employer, your environment. Inside, you have a self that is wanting to burst forth in truth, one that has been cultivated by your hopes, dreams, desires, passion, and pursuits, but there is the constant question that pops up, " Am I enough?"

There is a frustrated generation of Baby Boomers, Millennials, and rising culture of teens that are wondering if what they have and what they bring is enough to contribute to society. Their authentic inner self is struggling with the expectations that have been self and society imposed offering a pressure that is too heavy for them to wear on their shoulders.

Many of us take our entire lifetime attempting to find a place of security. Looking to the left and to the right settling in places we are allergic to. Like the pollen coating the Earth, we know that we should not stay in the places where we are now; but ANY place is better than NO place. The orphan spirit is a lonely spirit that needs affirmation because they never got it. Life is consistently unfulfilled.

Glitter and Gold

Everything that glitters is not gold. As we look to social media, magazines and other print media for answers to the questions that life brings, we will continue to be faced with the awesome task of choosing a lense for which to process the issues of life that we are faced with.

Are You Who You "Post" To Be?

For the person that is struggling with sexual identity, the sir who is now known as Catilyn may not be the best person that you should consult to help you find yourself. If you are trying to find a way to showcase your stuff in life,reality television may not be the best route to take. If you are trying to find what neighborhood in Atlanta, Beverly Hills, Australia, or another state to live in, reality television may not be the way to go.

For years, we have looked externally to attempt to resolve our issues. After hiding his emotional issues for years, he has now, with the help of media, found a way to share his story of desperately needing to come forth in his truth that he is transgendered and wants to dress as a woman. I believe that whether 12 or 65, if you have not dealt with your issues and the real issues that led to you wanting to exhibit that behavior, you will NEVER walk in your truth' rather, you will be exalted to become a role model for the masses while you are actively needing to process your abuse, hurts, and wounds that caused your pain and need to retreat.

As much as I love the actors that are on reality television, I believe that the showcase of them coming on shows to act out scripted issues that plague culture, it will only seek to continue to entertain people and never serve as a showcase of best practices that can be used recover a nation. Yes, I know, reality television is about profit and those watching are grown and can make their decision to do so or not. Yes, this is true, however, I'd simply like to provide insight after realizing that when life gets tough, we retreat and wrapping ourselves up in the lifestyle of another can indirectly cause us to want to emulate that same behavior or lifestyle for ourselves; even when many of us cannot afford it.

If you have followed my work through the years, you would know my 2nd book called, "Overcoming the Orphan Spirit: Restoration for Self and Society", is a book about identity and the orphan spirit. You can pick up your copy right now on Amazon (http://www.amazon.com/Overcoming-Orphan-Spirit-Restoration-Society/dp/1497434815). Overcoming the Orphan Spirit: Restoration for Self and Society encourages you to examine if you are dealing with the orphan spirit and how to identify areas in your life that may be hindering you from coming into the knowledge and embrace of Father God's love for you.

The love that God has for us transcends societal qualifications and performance criteria, it is simply receiving the love that God has for you. This book is an invitation to those who may have known their Creator for years or those who are in a baby step knowledge of Him. Either way, I share my personal tragedies and triumphs to encourage you to accept the Father's embrace. He loves you, always has and always will!

As mentioned in the book, the orphan is attracted to the presence of a thing because the external surface of things has always been the existence of the orphan. Craving for a whiff of the internal, the orphan desires to give themselves to something, anything to instill security into their spirit. As the root of the orphan spirit is abandonment, rejection, anger, pain, isolation, and a deep sense of regret.

From the time you flip the pages of the magazines or log onto social media channels, you are immediately faced with what I like to call "glitter". For anyone that has seen or been in a "glitter" storm, it can be raining outside with the weather thundering and lightning but pink glitter can make you believe that you are standing in the middle of sweet sunshine.

Imagine how the " enemy" comes in. You get the news that you are being laid off from work and rather than going home to tell your husband what has just happened so that you two can begin to adjust expenses and move things around, you log onto Instagram or Facebook Glitter and see a friend who has just purchased a new Tory Burch purse. Everything inside of you begins to cringe.

You start tearing up because you are immediately met with grief and the stages of grief are coming on you like rain. Suddenly, you are hit with the reality that your income has changed and your in need of collecting your thoughts but you decide to let them "go there".

Rather than taking the time to sit down and process what has happended, you drive to the nearest Tanger Outlet or mall and what do you do? You swipe that card and get that bag AND A WALLET with your bad self. Feeling a rush of energy and fulfillment, you post your bag and wallet on social media for all to see. The likes on Facebook turn into love on Instagram and you are in the zone. Days after, you realize that you are not going to get paid and you're toting around an empty purse with no money in it; not even two coins to rub together.

Glitter is so pretty, but it is such as distraction and can take you from the judgment that you know that you should follow. You know that buying a purse will not delete the emptiness that you feel in the core of your soul for losing your position, which for you represented and identity that is matchless; yet you went there for comfort. Glitter represents all that could come as a promise in life. When it is time for a cool breeze often called truth, the glitter disperses from the east to the west and that is where the healing, if you are ready, can begin.

It is so true what is said in John 10:10, "But the thief comes to ill, steal, and destroy, but I have come to give you abundant life." Trust me sister, it may not be today or tomorrow, but the day will come when you are able to go into that Tory Burch and purchase a bag that will be your with money overflowing. Until that time comes, go home and process your stuff.

Are You Who You "Post" To Be?

There will be now and until Jesus comes back, many things that will get in the way of focus. Buildings are erected all of the time for progress sake, but the sky still exists and has for some time. We can not allow the erection of a building, a person, a job, money, food, drugs, sex, and other stuff to distract us from the person that we are supposed to be. Can we pause from being the person that we post to be to focus on the person that we were intended to be?

Human behavior will tell you that in this world, we are constantly moving. Things rarely stop moving so that they can regenerate. Think of the caterpillar, think of the acorn, the process of sowing and reaping; if these things move and evolve, surely you should know that we are, as people, supposed to continue to evolve. As much as we would like it to be the case, we will go through changes in this life that will alter our appearance; we may get pregnant and have children leading to sagging breasts, we may encounter an allergic reaction that may cause a rash that can heal, we may encounter a hair change or whatever it is, we may alter our physical appearance, but please KNOW THIS, our identity in Christ is the ONLY fixed thing that we can know for sure.

I share with many of my clients why it is so important at this intersection of our lives, that we may God as the center of our being. Jobs are pink slipped, cars are wrecked or returned, relationships evolve, money moves, homes get renovated, and the like, but when we loose or grow from those things, the love of Father God will always be there so it is for our best that we make him the center of our being.

At the core of all of us, there is a core self that is WAITING, CRYING OUT, HOPING, for an introduction to you. If you get still, and ask God to speak to you, he will begin to do an awesome work of introducing you to the person of your core and revealing the true desires of your heart. So then, the question becomes, now who am I now, but what at this point in my life, would I like to experience?

Are You Who You "Post" To Be?

It is then that we realize, the pressure of trying to answer the whys of growing tired with our self or addressing the frozen places in our life don't and why they don't yield a reward of clarity for addressing them, become replaced with a focus on trying to put ourselves out there to experience new things: couponing, painting, writing, singing, bingo, or setting up a facebook page on social media.

A snapshot selfie can no longer hold you in a time warp.

The Intervention

Doing the Work

Stuck in time, unwilling to realize, unwanting to understand that we can move forward from our pain, hurts, failures, mistakes, we too can learn that we can achieve greatness and move on to become all that God has intended for us to be.

There is woman somewhere who is getting up from the sex stanked sheets of a one night stand……..

Somewhere, the women who found embrace in the arms of another woman due to multiple rapes that remained hushed hushed in her home is sending a thank you card to her former lover because she is returning back to her first love….Jesus…….

Are You Who You "Post" To Be?

The woman who is sitting in the closet taking a hit of the pipe while burying her head in her hands because she knows that the pipe can not give her a high like God can but she has messed up so much it was better to just continue that break free. She now breaks free...........

My sister who was abused by her father and after telling your mom you were ignored and forever silenced. Such a brutal act for your heart, mind, and body to endure, you have reached the point of knowing that being alone will not help you. You are going to stop punishing yourself for what was done to you and forgive yourself and move forward, letting Father God love on you and that man who loves you so much now, stop making him pay for the mistakes of your biological father. Receive the love and let it flow.

Think for one moment about the women in the bible who had the issue of blood. OMG! SO much blood, and we think our time of the month, which for some, ranges from 3-5 days is a task.....can you imaging bleeding for 12 years. My goodness, she had to have a line item for personal hygiene items and Tylenol! Too MUCH!!!! For the majority of that time, she decided to stay at home and be with herself often lacking the company of others which created a deep sense of loneliness. That constant bleeding no doubt caused her to be anemic, weak, and moody, called unclean, and low on funds, she needed help and wanted to be free. You can read all about this chick in (Luke 8:43-48). One encounter with Jesus Christ freed her from her bleeding and gave her an awesome quality of life, all because she was tired of the way in which she was operating and wanted to break free.

Once she got free, I am sure that she made have found herself asking, " Well, who am I now?" I am not going to be a regular customer on the hygiene and medicine aisle at Walmart, I will not be a regular patient at the doctor's office, I will not be able to remain with the ones who are still in an "unclean"state, who am I now? While excited about the possibility and potential of who she is going to become as a result of her healing, she can not focus on that as of yet because she is weighed down about the ones the she is leaving behind, or the baggage of where she came from. Does she take that baggage with her into her new state, does she leave it behind?

What does she do with her stuff now? If you ever been a caretaker to anyone, you know, it is best to take it all cause you never know if you'll need it in the future, but trust me, when you are FOCUSED in KNOWING that you have been HEALED FOREVER by the Lord Jesus Christ, you will NOT need to take the MESS from your past into where he is trying to take you next. Trust me, if you have a little menstrual during the journey or whatever, you best believe that MY GOD will supply so this is a message to all of my sisters out there: LEAVE IT BEHIND..........

The sex stained sheets......LEAVE IT!

The funky expensive perfume he bought you.......LEAVE IT!

The car that he is holding over your head for tricks..........LEAVE IT!

The job that you have to give head to keep..............LEAVE IT GIRL!!!!!!

Now that you have tapped into your core self and Jesus himself, learn to be instructed from the new experiences that you will face. You have permission to experience new experiences.

Despite all of the STUFF that we are hearing in the churches today, I want you to know that Jesus still heals delivers, and sets people free. He is still able to speak to you about your situation and put you on the path to wholeness NO MATTER how long you have been sitting in your mess.

HE is and STILL does desire to make you whole. You gotta know that sista! Pressing into your healing by running after the one who can give it to you rather than posting it on social media or running after things that will only temporarily give your relief, will assure you that wholeness will be yours. Them that keep their mind stayed on YOU GOD will have perfect peace (Isaiah 26:3).

The unclean, broken, and messed up are often separated and left to wallow in their mess. TD Jakes, one of my favorite preachers of all time stresses that people with issues tend to " Colonize" in groups to amplify and perpetuate their issues. When we are wallowing in our mess, we do not leave any room for God to do what he wants to do through the grace of Jesus Christ in faith to be made whole. That grace is available, free, and powerful to break every chain in your life.

Abandonment, death, grief, separation, may hurt and sting a lot as well as take time to heal from but you can.

From those experiences you will wonder yet again who am I now that I am unpartnered or unmothered. I want to encourage you that you, even in the pain of it all, will begin to take the steps to develop clarity about recrafting your new sense of self.

Along the way, you may run into your girlfriends that profess that you need to get with the program because unlike you, they know themselves so well.....LIES! Trust me, anyone who has to take the time to make you feel like crap at the expense of their happiness are not sure about who they are! TRUST ME!

First let's take the time to unload that something has happened to you first of all. You did experience a loss, a separation, a death which has put you in the state of searching that you are now in. What does that look like for you now? Take a few moments to write down what that means to you?

_____

_____

_____

_____

_____

_____

_____

Know that you have explained what this means to you, are you ready to verbalize and write down what you are now as a result of the situation? For instance, December 2013, before the birth of my recent baby, we lost a beautiful baby that left us feeling deeply hurt and sad for a long time. I had to get to the point at that time to say that my current state was <u>unmothered.</u>

So know that I have shared my state at that time, I'd like to ask you what is your current state: (write it below in one word or in as many words as you need to).

You see, I had to verbalize it and write it down so that I could reach the point of giving that to God and asking him to help me in my brokenness because I am unmothered. So with you, you may be reading this part in the book and find that at this very moment, you are not quite ready to face this part of your life (and that is okay). You can skip over, dog ear, or bookmark this section until you are ready. Once you find that you are, it will be time to present this to God and ask him to help you to identify who you are now.

As you move through this process, know that at this point in your life, if you knew everything, there would be no need to grow so take the time to get to know your core, take the time to know Father God. In all of our days of going to church, many of us find ourselves unchurched because we never got the chance or took the time to get to know him for ourselves. Trust me sister, it is high time. While you are going through this phase, let me say the favorite saying who's author's name I am not certain of but it says, " Blessed are the flexible for they will never be bent out of shape. " See this journey as a process and not as a burdensome task. The ebb and flow of discovering yourself will show you what needs to say and what should go, what can be strengthened, and what should not stay.

The Truth About Breakthroughs

Many have said, "I'll know it when I see it" but often breakthroughs come at the most inopportune times of our life. Just when we think we have dotted every me and crossed every t, we realize that what we thought was the will of God for us was actually us ordering our own steps and gliding off of a performance oriented mindset.

Getting a breakthrough is not like ordering takeout. You are not always able to choose the menu as you'd like. There is often a plate of test and confusion that gets served before the blessing arrives, often the calm before the storm. The question becomes, "Can you serve a God that hears your prayers but may not deliver your blessing in a perfect pink box?" What if that box is filled with masking tape, bruised and damaged from the journey to its destination, to you? Will you know it when it came and receive it with open arms?

One of my favorite artists, Laura Story, recently discussed on YouTube how she was going through a season in her life in writing the songs for her recent album. In the middle of writing the songs, she discovered that she was pregnant with twins and that her husband had a brain tumor. Faced with the decision to cave in, quit, or keep pressing, she wrote one of the most powerful songs ever that speaks to the form in which our blessings may choose to arrive. If we are not careful we can miss it because it may not come in the prettiest form that we are expecting.

Are You Who You "Post" To Be?

My personal breakthrough came when coming smack dab in the middle of my recent grief. For those of you that have followed me over the years, I speak about the orphan spirit and how God delivered me from the clutches of this spirit that causes a deep seated sense of abandonment and reliance on self to perform until exhaustion without coming to understand the liquid love that Father God has for us. Take a moment and ask Father God to empty you, comfort, you and prepare you. Now write what is being revealed to you right now.

_____

_____

_____

_____

_____

The Confrontation

"Did you really mean to say that?" Well, yes I did. There are some things in this life that will have to have confrontation when it happens. Most of us are sitting in the sit of regret knowing that something has happened to us that has offended, violated, hurt, and impacted us but for whatever reason, we decided to not handle the situation. Whether it was a single isolated event or a scandal, we decided to remain silent now we are reaping the heat of anger and carrying the weight of regret wanting to confront an issue or a person that is aged over with molded cheese.

"How do you tell someone that has gone on with their life as if nothing ever happened that for the last ten years+ you have been carrying pain or hurt?" Thinking that they or others may look upon you with laughter or blowing off, you suppress it and hold it till you are forced to take prescription meds to function through life. This is NOT God's best for you.

Pearls Before Swine

I know, I know, you want to tell them all what happened to you. You want someone, anyone, to listen to the pain that you went through. When Jesus spoke about the pearls before swine speech he was reminding us to stop putting our valuable things before people who do not appreciate them. As a people, we are made for relationship. For many people, the idea of having relationships online makes up for not having tangible relationships that we can converse or chill with. Afterall, a web cam these days makes us believe that ANYTHING is possible.

The Savior Syndrome is rampant in society today because many are looking to be rescued while many are seeking to lift themselves out of their issues to rescue others.

The ministry of helps has found its way to the world of social media and as a result, the cycle of abuse, aggression, and drama is at an all time high.

Why do we resort to this type of behavior? Could it be that we are orphans and never found our identity in the one who could truly take the pain away? Rather than posting who we want to be on social media, we should have been consulting with the one who could make us over from what were are into what we should be.

I hope that you will join me on my Monday night free webinars that are called " Essential Truths About Your Identity". One the webinars, we talk about the core principles associated with establishing, and for some, re-establishing our identity in Jesus Christ.

Believe it or not, the first orphan was Lucifer himself, also known as Satan. In the book of *Isaiah 14:13-14:*

Are You Who You "Post" To Be?

"You said in your heart,

I will ascend to the heavens;

I will raise my throne

above the stars of God;

I will sit enthroned on the mount of assembly,

on the utmost heights of Mount Zaphon.

I will ascend above the tops of the clouds;

I will make myself like the Most High."

It goes onto to tell us in the book of *Ezekiel 28:17* it says,

"Your heart became proud

on account of your beauty,

and you corrupted your wisdom

because of your splendor.

So I threw you to the earth;

I made a spectacle of you before kings."

Many of us have not grown up in a family where plans were made for us before we were born or to have the knowledge of being happy as a regular thing. Knowing from the beginning that we were created in the image of God is a valuable tool that can save you time and energy so that you can focus on attaining the purpose.

Sadly for many, when you look at Maslow's Hierarchy of Needs, you see that at the bottom of the triangle (as shown in the example),

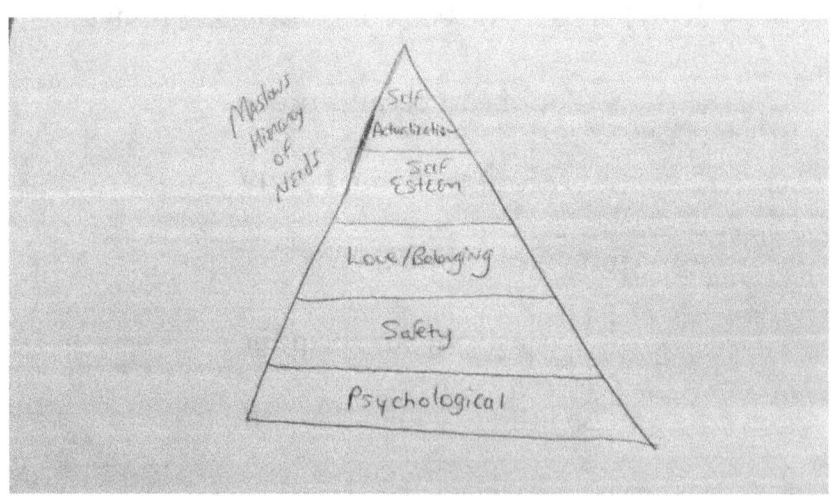

Are You Who You "Post" To Be?

Looking at this chart may provoke some questions in your mind about your current mindset. Let's take the time to answer a few questions about our needs:

1. What are the top 3 needs that you felt were achieved in your childhood? In reverse of that, what are the top 3 needs that you believe were not achieved in your childhood?

    _____

    _____

    _____

    _____

2. Now, let's answer those same two questions for present day? Today, what are the top 3 needs that you believe are being met in your life right now? What are the top 3 needs that are not being met in your life right now?

    _____

    _____

    _____

    _____

Is there some part of you that believes are still a struggle for you or are causing you to remain "stuck" in a childhood mentality? In what ways would you want to have them met?

_____

_____

_____

_____

Many of us turn to social media because there have been wounds that have gone unhealed for years. Maybe we did not get the validation from our father or mother and as a result we are unsure of how and what to do when authenticity shows up: do we embrace or run away from it. For as much as I talk about the Fatherhood of God to adopt us and bring us into his own, there is also a nurturing Motherhood of God that can heal those mommy issues that we remain unhealed from.

I thought it was amazing to view the Facebook video several weeks ago where mothers were sitting in chairs and random children were blindfolded and asked to identify their mother. It was so touching to see the instinctual nature of these children to know their mothers by a touch of the face, a whisper of a voice, or a smell of soap on the skin. It brought tears, a running river of tears to my eyes, because I wondered if the number of women, like myself, who lost their mother years and years ago, would be able to pick their mother out blindfolded after all of these years.

For many of us, our relationship with our mother was our first introduction to the expressed love. From the time we were in the womb of our mother, although tumultuous at times, she had a way to bring stillness, serenity, and comfort to us. For many that was not your experience and for that I am so sorry. I know that despite what you went through or how you God here, you can be, now, eternally loved by Father God.

When you do not know the purpose of a thing, it is inevitable that abuse will be present. There are so many directions that pain can take us as a people, society, and culture. Many women endure the pain of female genital mutilation at the hands of oppression from a people that do not understand their power. Shredding a female's vagina often without anethsia will not delay sexual passions. It will hurt and rob the young female of her virtue now.

We know that just as Satan, the enemy is a thief, if he has a Facebook account, he would not like anything the woman does. From the Garden of Eden to the understanding that every woman will gain as a result of reading the bible and books like this to build them up, the he will continue to hate any woman who walks in the sweet intimacy that comes with being a woman. So because of this, get your issues right with your mother, with your sister, Satan has ruled us for far too long, let us reject him rather than each other with our self imposed, driven by media, we cannot get along syndrome.

www.water.org reported recently that the lack of water is the number global risk based on impact to society today. There are approximately 750 million people that lack access to safe water.

The Bureau of Labor Statistics reported that 8.3 million people in the United States are unemployed. Although this figure has risen by 375,000 over the past two months, the amount is still staggering and represent real people.

Realty Trac reported that between 2007 and 2011, there were more than 4 million foreclosures completed and 8.2 million foreclosure starts.

Maslow's hierarchy of needs is a great indicator as to where we are a people. If we are trying to get our basic needs met like shelter and food, maintain or secure employment, keep our home secure, and have a secure sense of self, who we are both as a friend and partner, how can we achieve our highest best self? This is the reason why I love Oprah and all the thought leaders that follow happiness psychology because I refuse to believe the will for our lives rest in consistently being downtrodden and gloomed.

I believe that it is possible to achieve self-actualization in this life once we clear our lives of the cluttered and filters of our past. Satan was an orphan so he wanted to become like God and began to behave and deceive so that he could acquire a tribe under him to continue his mission. We do not have to be in his tribe any longer. We can accept the fact that we have been asleep but our eyes have become awaken to purpose and we are ready to embrace our stuff, get healed from our past wounds, and get adopted by Father God.

When we are adopted, we must begin to look inward rather than outward. My webinar last week included a teaching on the Savior Syndrome. There I talked about how we tend to utilize outward tools to communicate our pain. There comes a time, when our healing must be turned inward and not focused on those who can give us a handout or an ear to listen. Even if the spirit of abandonment is overtaking you right now, you must know that Psalms 27:10 is true, " For my father and mother have forsaken me, but the Lord will take me up."

Are you ready to lay Instagram down and throw a picture of your imperfect mother or father or self before Father God? Are you ready for the great transfer?

- **For your mother /father, say this.....**Momma/Daddy (or the woman/man who I respectfully call as the one who birthed/fathered me), I am feeling a lot of emotions right now and attempting to get clarity, no matter where I am right now, I know that I must forgive to free myself from anymore pain. Maybe you were suffering from your own stuff, but you never gave me the love I felt I needed. When I wanted you to love on me and cheer for me, your chided me with your words and that really hurt. You never took the time to look at me other than to tell me how much you disliked me or my actions, this really hurt me. Today, through the power of Jesus Christ, I have been adopted and he is helping me to recover and resolve all of these issues in my heart. I want you to know that I forgive you for not being what I needed you to be in my life. You did not open your heart to me and I forgive you for this as well. You simply did not have it to give to me so I release you from that right now. In the name of Jesus, amen.

I realize that saying this may stir up much in you right now. Please take the time to express yourself:

_____

_____

_____

_____

_____

Now, as the bible declares there is rest when we come to the end of ourselves and attempting to fix and solve the things in life that are too great for us. Now that we have been able to get beyond this, are you ready to invite Father God to come in?

Say this to Father God..........You have always been there loving on me. Before my mother gave birth to me, you were there loving on me and letting me know that you knew me. I have just surrendered the painful thought of my mother or father not wanting me and I need you know to embrace me as your child. Help me to forgive in wholeness and not just half heartedness. For all of the things that I have attempted to use to fill the void that only you can fill, I am so sorry and ask that you clean up the space that belongs to you. Come in and live there. Wash me with the water of your word and cleanse my mind and behavior. I trust you to meet every present and future need that I have Father God. In the name of Jesus, amen.

(Visit *danitaogandaga.com* for more information on our 7 week Group Coaching Program beginning February 2016. Also visit our store to purchase the Kindle or print edition of *Overcoming the Orphan Spirit* and audio recording of the 7 *Habits of Highly Effective Orphans* to help you understand more about healing from deep wounds from the orphan spirit.)

The Restoration

Mindsets: The Conditions of Our Minds

Before we begin this chapter, I'd encourage you to take a few moments and examine the question, "With everything that may be occurring in your world right now, what you know to be true?" I know it sounds like the biggest cliché especially since we hear it and read it on Oprah and Jet Magazine, but really examine this question as we delve into this chapter.

There is an expensive price on saying yes to change and to being different and most importantly, to following your purpose. For anyone who has attempted to go against the grain of life, the one directional movement that society and culture direct us towards, this chapter is for you. I am sure by now, you have been able to, inspite of your battle scars and wounds say that it was all worth it in making the decision to doggedly go where the average man could not or would not go. When you choose to follow the will of God for your life, there is an immediate separation and equipping that takes place where you realize that the journey may not be what you want it to be but in the end it will be about bringing glory to God.

I am glad that I can write these faith filled words to you know, because a couple of years ago, every fiber of my being was challenged in trying to believe and accept the call that God has placed on my life. I was raised by two Baptist preachers and taught that education was the key to success. When both of my parents passed away in my twenties, I busied myself with getting filled with education.

As result, opportunities came from every direction to ensure my success in that area from teaching at a university at the age of 24 to working as a non-profit consultant writing grants to revive an economically challenged community in the City of Pittsburgh, Pennsylvania. In a matter of a year, God had placed godly mentors in my life who ushered me to success and what I failed to realize that whole time, was that God had also began to work with me on healing the issues of my heart.

Whatever we give ourselves to in this life is what we will become full of and for me, I choose to become fuller of the world system of success than that of the Kingdom of God. For years, I went through the motions of paying my tithes because mama said, going to church every Sunday, because mama said, and reading Psalms 25 and 27, because mama said but after a while I realized that something was missing.

It took my good friend at the time, Darcy Ogandaga coming to visit me for me to realize that everything that I thought I had acquired in this life at this age was only by the grace of God and for me to be able to survive and gain the healing that I desperately needed in life, I would have to seek more of God and his will for my life. I remember when Darcy came to visit me, the first thing we did after dinner on his first day visiting me was watch a VHS tape by Pastor Creflo Dollar called, " No More Lack". I began looking at Darcy saying, "Darcy, I do not have lack, I am 25 years old making good money with a good job and great place to live and a car, I do not have lack!"

He was smiling at me the whole time and inserted the tape into the player. Let's just say when that message ended, I was in a bath of tears because I realized that it did not matter how much material things that I had accumulated, there was still an enormous amount of pain that existed in my life due to the loss of my parents that I did not address. As a result, the treadmill of performance gave me great comfort because I could wake up every day and put on a mask to perform in the area I was trained to excel in and function at the top of my game, commanding respect, attention, and advisement wherever I go, but in the academic and corporate arena, no one, absolutely no one was concerned about the condition of your heart just ensuring that the community has what it needed to survive.

Wow, the truth of that causes me to pause while writing this book because I realize that this is exactly the place that millions of people are in at this very moment, dressing up in their finest clothes going about their well-paid jobs, driving their fast cars, and living in the elitist zip codes but in the night, they scream silently, consuming wine, pop prescription or OTC pills and consume other spirits to help them sleep through the night, bawled up like a baby wanting to get back into their mother's womb....essentially orphaned and in need of a savior.

The Little Green Book: Starbuck's Perspective

If you have followed me on social media, you know that one of my favorite hangouts is the Starbucks in my local community. It is the place where I come to on evenings and weekends with my children to have a cup of coffee or tea and talk with friends. It is a place where my husband and I get together to strategize and pray about the increasing our businesses. I often do initial client pop-ins at this location. It is simply an amazing place to congregate.

In an effort to pay attention to the quality versus the consumption of customers based on quantity, Starbucks, developed The Little Green Book which as I researched was a way to continuously monitor the maintenance of the mission and values that went into creating the company. The green book serves as a pocket size guidebook to understand how decisions are made,   problems are handled, as well as how to create an atmosphere of teamwork.

Many would say, "What is the point of a green little book?" Similar to this, we teach our 5 year old who was 4 at the time how to confess the word over everything that she believed for and many wondered why focus on teaching her this so young? The importance of building a foundation of being clear about where you help comes from is essential to living a fulfilled life.

If you are certain about where your help comes from, you will not look to people to give you what they are unable to or to fill you up when you are empty. I heard it best from my husband who once told me, "People are merely a resource, but remember that God is your source!" Think about that for a moment. There is something about establishing yourself in writing your foundational beliefs out long hand on paper. Habakkuk 2:2 says for us to write the vision and to make it plain. I believe that confession works and is essential to life.

While we are purchasing magazines, listening to audio and e-books, or going onto social media to remind us of our value, let us continue to remember that there is a book that provides us with the affirmation that we need to knowing our true identity in a world that consistently tries to define and redefine it for us. So many people in the world are without a foundation and if they ever had one, it has been cracked and never repaired, and because of this, their entire perspective for living life is cracked. People like this are hungry for sight and in need of a new way to view things.

Know that with everything that we do in life, there is a process. Whatever it is that you are coming out of, remember that there is going to be steps that you will need to take to develop a new mindset. "How does it happen for some people, but not to me?" This may be a question that you have asked yourself for years and still doubting or unsure that you can come out of your mindset.

Yes, you can come out of your mindset. I am not going to say that formulas fix because we all know that they do not. According to www.directselling411.com , 15.6 million people are involved in the direct selling business in the United States. I am sure that while this number is huge, there are formulas that may be associated with the success of the companies that they are involved in; yet the success of each of the 15.6 million people cannot be guaranteed because it is up to the individuals to create their own success utilizing the tools that have been given to them via the companies.

Similarly, with our healing and the mindsets that we chose to have, it is a decision that we must make to get the hearing that we are in need of in order to move from victim to victor, from brokenness to healed, from painful to prosperous. What does that look like, you must ask? I am glad you asked. As with anything, we must take the time to count the cost.

Adopt Me

Before you decide to do anything, I want you to examine who is at the center of your life? When you take an

73

apple and core it from the inside what do you find on the inside? When we core you, what will we find? Is it your car, house, job, husband or boyfriend, or that shoe collection that is holding you together? It is essential that we answer this question because that will determine the current state of how you are viewing life. When you lost your father due to an illness or when your father never showed up for your track meet, how did you process that?

A recent message from my pastor put things in perspective for me recently about how we must develop a new lense. There is so much taking place in the world in which we live that it is imperative that we take a moment to think about what is holding us together. I remember going through the painful loss of my parents almost 17 years ago. Since the loss happened in my early twenties, I was met with all types of questions about my identity, who I was going to love, should I love a man or a woman, should I get high so that I could not face the pain, maybe I should find someone to love me like my dad and sure enough, these questionings led me down a path that did not have to occur but I went down fast trying to find answers to life's questions.

Whatever your path maybe, taking the time to make Jesus the center of your being is critical because when life comes with its twists and turns, you will need something greater than yourself to hold you up when you feel like caving in and quitting on life. It will be essential to allow the Father to heal you and help you. Taking the time to get adopted is essential to receive the unconditional love of Father God. His love can come in and repair the breach that exists from not receiving the love from your father or mother during the formative years of your life where you should have known that someone loved you or felt cared for.

Father God is saying to you, "I know that your Father and Mother may have abandoned you, but I am here. Allow me to come in and adopt you, let me love on you." I encourage you to meditate on the following scriptures that helped me during the rough time of rebuilding my identity in Christ and not through the loss of my mother and father. Loss follows and lives with rejection, isolation, and despair. The peace of Father God will make you whole if you reach out to him.

- Before you were conceived, I knew who you were...........................Jeremiah 1:4-5

- I knew the exact time of your birth and where you would be placed............Acts 17:26

- I know how many hairs are on your head (even without the sew-ins).............Matthew 10:29-31

Renew My Strength

Walking out of one mindset and into another and often going through the task of realizing that you have fronted, skeemed, or faked it can be shameful but I encourage you to not allow the enemy to keep you in that space as you face your truth.

Are you ready:

Step One: Look very closely at this picture

Who are you now?

_____

_____

_____

_____

_____

Do you like what you see?

_____

_____

_____

_____

_____

So today, you may answer no, you do not like who you see and that is fine. It is truth in need of adjustment. As you go through the days to come, I encourage you to ask Father God to remind you of who you are in him. Allow his words to be the only words that you hang on to. Trying to call up Tyrone or boyfriends from the past to affirm us or give us value will not do because long after they lost your number, I am sure their opinion of you changed as well.

Remember the following scriptures:

- **Jeremiah 1:5** "I knew you before I formed you in your mother's womb. Before you were born I set you apart and appointed you as my prophet to the nations"

- **John 1:12** "Yet to all who received him, to those who believed in his name, he gave the right to become children of God"

- Ephesians 1:5 " He predestined us to be adopted as his sons through Jesus Christ, in accordance with his pleasure and will"

We have been given the power to take authority over the atmosphere. I did not understand the concept of the believer's authority until I was exposed to the teachings of great leaders such as Sarah Omakwu, Pastor Creflo Dollar, Kenneth Copeland, Joyce Meyer, Andrew Wommack, Bill Winston, and my husband, Darcy Ogandaga.

I used to hear it over and over that I cannot control the bird who flies over my head but I can ensure that he does not build a nest in my head. We hear euphemisms like this daily, but there is great truth in what we should allow to come into our mindset through our ear, eye, and mouth gates. Ask God to help you take authority over your mind and guard your heart in the days ahead.

Revisiting the Question

Now that we can say that our perspective has been changed, know that a cracked perspective calls for us to

- o Focus on the things that really do matter.
- o Realize that our healing from past hurts requires our immediate attention so that we

can focus our attention on receiving the liquid love from Jesus Christ and become free from the orphan spirit.

o Know that there is truth in Hebrews 13:8 says that Jesus is the absolute same yesterday, today, and forever. In Malachi 3:6 God expressed himself, "For I am the Lord, I do not change.

So, I ask you once again, Who were you before the world told you what you were supposed to be? Are you who you " post" to be?

www.ingramcontent.com/pod-product-compliance
Lightning Source LLC
Chambersburg PA
CBHW070806290526
45795CB00002B/643